G P W

GPW as a young man (unsigned oil portrait)

George Parker Winship

AS LIBRARIAN · TYPOPHILE
AND TEACHER

Talks by Thomas R. Adams, Martin W. Hutner,
and Michael B. Winship,
delivered in the Memorial Rooms
of the Harry Elkins Widener Memorial Library
on April 17, 1997, together with a list
of students in Fine Arts 5e compiled
by Mariana S. Oller

Cambridge · The Harvard College Library

1999

Sixty-fifth through sixty-seventh
George Parker Winship Lectures
under the fund established by former members
of the John Barnard Associates

A Publication of the Microglyphics Fund

ISBN 0-914630-20-2

Contents

[v]

Foreword

Good afternoon. I'm Roger Stoddard, Curator of Rare Books in the College Library, glad to welcome you on behalf of my fellow college library officers to this meditation, so long overdue, on George Parker Winship. Never in my thirty-five years of Harvard Library service have I ever heard his name mentioned without respect, perhaps with awe; it has been my privilege to manage and introduce the lecture series endowed in his honor by his John Barnard Associates; but never has my curiosity about him been satisfied. Never have we concentrated our attention on man and deeds, his contribution to the work of the library and the life of the university, what he brought here for us, what he left for those of us who follow after. Today we do so, hard on the heels of another anniversary of the Titanic disaster.

"Cambridge at any time is full of ghosts" reminds the sage of Concord in his Journal. What better scene for summoning them back than this memorial room, sacred to the deceased young bibliophile, whose portrait mounted in mourning drapes and tassels dominates our gathering. Harry Widener's sad eyes follow us anywhere we go in this room, avoiding only the books he knew and loved and left behind in the great library,—"memorial to my dear son"—that his mother erected so proudly for him.

It is a good time to recall Commencement Day, June 24, 1915, as Bill Bentinck-Smith describes it: "Flanked by rows of the graduating senior class, and led by the President, the Governing Boards and the recipients of honorary degrees marched . . . through the Yard and up the Library steps to the doors of the building. Here Mrs. Widener presented the keys to Mr. Lowell, and then the procession moved into the Library and up the staircase to the Widener Room. Archibald Coolidge, among the first, was carrying the surviving volume of John Harvard's donation, Downame's *The Christian warfare.* . . . Senator Lodge spoke movingly regarding the spirit of Mrs. Widener's gift. President Lowell responded. Bishop Lawrence offered a prayer and benediction. . . ."

Just think of them climbing up the thirty steps, beneath the stone-carved Harvard book-labelled seal flanked by the torches of knowledge relayed, passed on, and the marks of the first printers — Fust and Schoeffer (Gutenberg's successors), Aldus (symbolic printer of Renaissance), Caxton (who carried the torch to England), and Rembolt (who bore it in Paris), up the twenty-one steps to the landing, through the doors into the Rotunda and then the Memorial Room — most of the ascent under the sad gaze of Harry Widener from his portrait.

But, loss, mourning, and sadness enclose this space, and the aftermath of young Widener's tragic death brought sadness also. The great American bookman Luther Livingston had been chosen curator. "He loved you, Mr. Livingston, and has talked to me so often of your knowledge and the help you were to him in advising him about books," wrote Mrs. Widener, "Hundreds of times he has told me, that when he could afford it, he would love to have you for his private librarian. You were so congenial with him and he loved working with you." On the very day of the Titanic disaster Livingston was taken by the illness that eventually extinguished him: he visited the half-completed library in commencement week, 1914, sat in his wheelchair at the speaker's table during the Phi Beta Kappa dinner, received his corporation appointment on November 30, died within a month, and was buried from Appleton Chapel.

"Livingston's remarkable memory for minute details and his ability to recognize peculiarities in volumes with which he was unfamiliar had long been an important asset," wrote GPW, a description you will hear echoed in a later account of William Jackson, who carried on the work, "a natural bibliographer with an immense capacity to recall the physical and bibliographical details of copies of books he had seen." Winship it was who succeeded Livingston, who planned the commencement ceremonies in the Memorial Room, who flourished here while providing much joy to others, — some of it at the table over there — and left with sadness for all.

You have some background, some thumbnail biographies in a conference paper of mine, printed for this occasion, "Teaching the History of Books at Harvard." Help yourselves to copies. Today I quote a single, additional source. Arthur A. Houghton Jr. with his brilliant, tough mind, was easily unimpressed with the experiences of life, but here he offers a vivid recollection in his *Remembrances* (1986): "I took . . . a bibliographical course under George Parker Winship. I had already started collecting books, looked with reverence at the titles behind glass in the Harry Elkins Widener Room, and spent my allowance at the rare book shops Lauriats and Goodspeeds in Boston. Not daring to go back to my father for funds, I had to sell my winter overcoat to Max Keezer, the second-hand clothing dealer in Cambridge, to pay my book bill at Lauriats. It was all so heady and exciting that I could hardly stand it. Harvard did much, much for me."

This afternoon speakers have come to do much, much for us from far Providence, New York City, and Austin. Each has accepted responsibility for an aspect of GPW's life and career. We thank them every one — but now, I cede the lectern to three colleagues who will introduce the speakers: the Roy E. Larsen Librarian of Harvard College, Nancy M. Cline; the Honorary Curator of Modern Typography, Charles A. Rheault; and, the Curator of the Harry Elkins Widener Memorial Rooms, Virginia L. Smyers.

In the Widener Memorial Room
April 17, 1997

George Parker Winship:
The Providence Years.

BY THOMAS R. ADAMS

Librarian Emeritus of the John Carter Brown Library.

On October 26th of 1894 a young assistant in the Harvard History Department wrote a letter to Justin Winsor, the Librarian of Harvard College.

"MY DEAR DR. WINSOR:

"American history began to interest me in my Sophomore year in college (1890−91), when I worked up the school history of Massachusetts before 1650, in connection with Professor Channing's course of lectures in colonial history. In connection with this work, I succeeded in handling a good many of the rarer Americana in the college library, and also in the Massachusetts Historical Society Library. I printed some sketches of colonial schools, the result of this year's work, in the Boston *Journal of Education*.

"The next year I was working with Professor Hart, studying the history of the United States.

"I began my special study of the Spanish Explorations in my Senior year, taking up Coronado's Expedition to New Mexico and the Great Buffalo Plains, 1540−1542. After working through the collections of printed documents and the histories in the Harvard Library, I went to the Lenox Library in New York, where I was permitted through the courtesy of the Trustees, to copy the Spanish text of the Castañeda "Relacíon." Since then, I have translated this narrative and written a general historical introduction to this and other narratives of the Coronado Expedition. The whole is now ready for publication, and the history department is considering it. Three of the minor narratives have been printed, in my translation, two of them in the *American History Leaflets*, No. 13, and the other in the *Boston Transcript*.

"It was while I was doing this work on Coronado that I was thrown in contact with Dr. Feweks of the South-West-

ern Archaeological Expedition. You may recollect that they
talked of sending me to Spain to see what I could find —
Seville, and elsewhere, but the death of Mrs. Mary Hemen-
way ended this plan.

Partly in anticipation of this Spanish
trip, I prepared the list of documents relating to America,
contained in the *Colección de Documentos Inéditos*, which the
trustees of the Boston Public Library printed in the last number of their *Bulletin*.

"I received an appointment from the Harvard Corporation
a year ago this last September, as Assistant in American History, which appointment has been renewed for the current
year. This work has kept me in the college library a large
part of my time, and I have become familiar with the original
sources and material relating to American history down to
the adoption of the Constitution — and with the rarer works,
in order to prevent their destruction by too great use on the
part of undergraduate students.

"This fall I have had a little lecturing to do, besides, both
in the college and at Radcliffe.

"Besides this other work, last year I got a start on the
study of cartography, through lectures on the Geographical
Development of America, doing a little independent work
upon maps, in connection with Alarçon and Cortes voyages
up the Gulf of California. I also tried to find from the earlier
maps, how much information regarding Coronado's discover-
ies reached the map makers in Europe.

"As for myself, I was born in Bridgewater, Plymouth
County, in 1871 and was brought up there and in Somerville,
just outside Boston. I received my Harvard A. B. in 1893 and
my Master's degree last June.

GEORGE P. WINSHIP"

The letter was, in fact, a curriculum vitae for a job, and Winsor forwarded it immediately to Mr. John Nicholas Brown of
Providence, Rhode Island, who presided over the collection of
Americana which had been built by his father John Carter
Brown and himself. Beginning in 1865 the series of published
catalogues with their detailed descriptions and extensive
notes compiled by John Russell Bartlett had made its con-

tents known to the world. This was further enhanced by Justin Winsor's frequent references to the "Carter Brown Collection" in his *Narrative and Critical History of America* (1884–1889). It was not surprising then that the Browns were besieged by what today would be called reference questions. From 1853 to his death in 1886 John Russell Bartlett dealt with much of this correspondence. He also became a tutor to the Brown children. As such, one of his tasks was to introduce them, particularly the eldest John Nicholas Brown, to the library and the responsibilities that went with it. Young Mr. Brown on Bartlett's death wrote,

"His house was one where I used constantly to run in for a few minutes at a time (it was only a couple of blocks away) and now he is gone there is no one to take his place."

For a time the young man tried to cope, but he was the head of a family with many other interests and responsibilities. It became clear that the time had come to find someone to take Bartlett's place. A number of inquiries were made, including one about Herbert Putnam, the future Librarian of Congress. Finally Mr. Brown settled on Winsor's candidate. He got no ordinary employee. Following an initial interview Winship wrote him:

"Frankly, one reason I want to come to Providence and help you take care of the books you and your father have gathered . . . is that it seems to offer an unexampled chance for a young man to develop himself . . . as a student of American history . . . Most of all, I want to become sufficiently independent so that I shall not be tempted to print any serious writing I may do . . . until I am reasonably sure that no one will have to do the work over again. All this is the work and perhaps the attitude, for a mature man, but, if you are thinking of employing me, it is only fair that I should tell you of my ideals as well as my present equipment . . . I'm enough of a bibliophile to love and study books for their own sake, and can conceive of no better work for developing and maturing one's very best powers."

The position was offered and accepted. Winship had no intention of being a mere custodial librarian. Instead, he struck a bargain. In exchange for taking charge of Mr. Brown's library he would use it to further his career as an historian. The job began on May first 1895 and Winship immediately opened correspondence with three men who were to play an important part in his future. Henry Newton Stevens of Great Russell Street, London, was the son of Henry Stevens from whom John Carter Brown had made the major purchases that launched the library fifty years earlier. Relations between John Carter Brown and Henry Stevens had cooled at the end of the 1860s. Henry Newton Stevens was determined to renew them. Among other things he published Winship's second book. The second letter was to Wilberforce Eames, the librarian of the Lenox Library in New York City where Winship had come to know him when a graduate student. It was just at this time that the Lenox Library was being merged with the Astor Library and the Tilden Foundation to form the New York Public Library. There Eames emerged as the leading American bibliographer. For many years he served on the Visiting Committee of the John Carter Brown Library and in 1924 Winship, together with two younger colleagues, published his Festschrift, the first to honor an American bibliographer.

The third man to whom Winship wrote is less well known. But the letter was to have important consequences. It was to Frank Borton, a North American missionary school teacher in Puebla de los Angeles in Mexico who had written to Mr. Brown a couple of years before about Mexican books. Winship asked, "Can you tell us what has been done with the library of Señor Icazbalceta?" Joaquin García Icazbalceta, the Mexican historian and pioneer in the study of printing in Mexico, had died the previous November. Latin Americana was an area in which the Browns, father and son, had always collected and Winship's familiarity with Spanish and Spanish-American history may have been an important factor in his selection as librarian. The Icazbalceta library was not available but in February of 1896 Borton wrote that another important collection was coming up. It was the library of Dr.

Nicholas León, and it was reputed to be the best collection of Mexican books after Icazbalceta's. Borton undertook to act for Mr. Brown but negotiations dragged on through the spring and summer. Finally, in desperation, Borton wrote that the only way to settle things was to send Winship down with the money to deal directly with León. Borton hinted that Mexican, French, and Russian interests were in the picture. On September 11, Winship wrote to Mr. Brown from Mexico City:

"HAIL TO THEE—King that shalt be. I fear I am not wholly sober this evening despite the most careful abstinence. I have already telegraphed you that the purchase of Dr. León's Library is concluded, the books and receipt are in my possession, and the money, in his, $2,600.00 gold."

Within a year and a half of Winship's arrival the John Carter Brown collection had become supreme in yet another field of Americana. The year 1896 also saw the appearance of Winship's first major work, *The Coronado Expedition, 1540–1542*. It was published by the Bureau of Ethnology of the Smithsonian Institution. Still the authoritative work on the subject, it was reprinted in 1990.

During the next four years Winship carried out many of the same tasks that Bartlett had: dealing with booksellers, answering reference questions, and overseeing the library during Mr. Brown's frequent absences. He traveled abroad a good deal and was often in New York and in Newport. On one occasion Winship was asked to help select reading material for the crew of the Brown yacht. On another occasion he was asked to order two modern architecture books. This is the first hint that we have of Mr. Brown's plans to erect a separate library building behind the family home on Benefit Street.

It should be pointed out that Mrs. John Carter Brown did not transfer the legal ownership of the books to her son until his marriage in 1898. At that time he made a will setting out what was to happen to the library on his death. He had ambitious plans for the future and with Winship's help he was making important additions, such as assembling the most

complete collection of editions of Ptolemy's Geography. Mr.
Brown had never been a robust person. In March of 1900 he
attended the dedication of the new Providence Public Library
building to which he had made a major contribution. He
caught cold, it turned into typhoid fever, two weeks later he
died at the age of thirty-nine, and the will came into effect. It
provided that the Library, together with money to erect a
building and provide an endowment, was to be placed in the
hands of trustees who, in turn, were to select "some college,
university or other institution" to receive the Library under
the conditions of the trust. The most important of these conditions was that it should be maintained:

". . . AS A LIBRARY with its own separate and special housing,
library building, and to be kept separate and distinct from
any other library, with a special librarian."

What the inspiration for this provision was I do not know.
Perhaps the way in which the Lenox Library had been swal-
lowed up by the New York Public Library had something to
do with it. The plans for the library building were already
well advanced. In April of 1901 the Corporation of Brown
University accepted the conditions of the will and the building site was moved a few blocks away to the College Green.
Clearly Winship was a part of these negotiations. He reported to Stevens that:

"I THINK WE SHALL SUCCEED in securing a virtually independent management — although it may be necessary to ally
it directly with the University and call it a part of the University although not of the University Library."

Continuing in the employ of the family, he had his hands full.
Soon after the death of John Nicholas Brown, the younger
Brown brother Harold died leaving a significant collection on
the Church of England and the Episcopal Church. This was
added to the Library as the Harold Brown Collection of
Books on the History of the Church in America.

On the 29th of January 1904, the University appointed
Winship as Librarian. It was at this time that he managed
things so that the Library formally adopted the policy of re-

GPW in the John Carter Brown Library

GPW in the library of the Brown House

stricting itself to books relating to America printed before 1801. Nowhere can I find a statement by John Nicholas Brown limiting the Library to Americana or to imprints before 1801. On the contrary, in describing the Library he declares that it shall consist of the Bibliotheca Americana formed by his father:

". . . AND INCLUDING also any future additions of whatever nature I make hereafter thereto."

Already some notable incunabula had been bought and a few weeks before his death he wrote Winship of his hopes that General Rush Hawkins, who had married a cousin, Annmary Brown, would place his incunabula in the new building. These would fit nicely with a fine collection of Aldines which had been bought before John Carter Brown decided to concentrate on Americana. Thus at the outset George Parker Winship took control of the future direction of the library. Construction of the building began in October of 1902, and it was dedicated on May 17th 1904.

Initially Winship had to find a staff. One of the first people appointed was the binder, F. P. Hathaway. Selected by William Vail Kellen, a member of the Committee of Management, Hathaway was a talented craftsman, but he had a personality which conflicted with that of the librarian. Until the building of the recent addition a dent was visible in the basement wall where he threw a hammer at Winship. A most important addition to the staff came in 1907 when Winship hired Margaret B. Stillwell, later to be the curator of the Annmary Brown Memorial. Winship went on extended trips to Mexico and Cuba in 1911 and to Europe in 1913. On both occasions Miss Stillwell was left in charge and her long chatty letters detail the day-to-day activities of the Library. A delightful passage in her book, *Librarians are Human*, is the account of Winship's Irish setter which would lie under the Trustees' room table until his master dashed out the front door. The dog would leap up and follow him just squeezing through onto the porch before the heavy door closed. Another vignette comes from Miss Jean Richmond of Wakefield, R.I. She and two of her eight-year-old friends were roller skating on the porch and making an awful racket. The door opened and Winship stuck his head out and said:

"DON'T YOU WANT TO COME and see the pretty books? But first you must take your skates off."

Then there is the story about a small boy who was edging his way along the ledge at the back of the building. The window opened and Winship invited him in. Still another young man who got the "Winship treatment" was a Boy Scout bitten by the book bug — Albert Lownes, whose great collection on the history of science is now in the John Hay Library at Brown.

Winship decided that the JCB was an ideal platform from which — in his own words — to "culturate Providence." Receptions for visiting dignitaries, small parties, entertainments for clubs and student groups — anything which would explain the Library to the community, were part of the Librarian's program. Internally, to get the collection organized, he devised a classification scheme which was so sophisticated that it probably would have required a computer to have completed the job in less than two or three lifetimes.

There was, however, a much bigger job of selling. The John Carter Brown Library was, to Winship, an institution of national and even international importance, and he set out to see that it played an appropriate role. He was active in the affairs of the American Antiquarian Society, and one summer he taught at the University of California at Berkeley. His participation in the work of the American Historical Association is particularly interesting. Ray Allen Billington in his "Tempest in Clio's Teapot" described the rebellion in 1915 of members of the Association against:

"TWO OR THREE DOZEN PROFESSORS from a half-dozen universities, drawn largely from those in their senior years . . . within this governing clique an elite inner core known as the 'Nucleus Club' met annually at a gay champagne dinner where fundamental policy decisions were made — or so the masses of the members believed."

Winship, who had no PhD and no faculty rank, was a part of

this inner group and was frequently responsible for arranging the dinners.

We must not, however, lose sight of the fact that Winship's most important task was to build the collections. In September of 1904 he purchased Peter Martyr's *Libretto de tutta la Navigatione,* Venice 1504, the second and only perfect copy of the first printed account of Columbus's second and third voyages. Winship was not averse to buying expensive books, but that was not his long-range vision for the Library. In 1907 a member of the Committee of Management suggested that with some major collections of great rarities coming up for auction it might not be wise to spend money on a large number of less expensive things. To this he replied:

"WE RECEIVED FROM MR. BROWN a collection of rare books. In three years — and with thirty thousand dollars — my personal opinion is that it has become a well rounded collection of material on a large number of subjects — on several of which it is today unrivaled . . . If this policy is right — the book for which we pay $15 or $2 is likely to be as useful and as important as that for which we pay a thousand."

Winship collected remarkably cheaply. Areas he attacked that had not yet attracted much attention were early cosmography and geography, the West Indies (where he assisted the pioneer bibliographer of the West Indies Frank Cundall), and the political pamphlets of the American Revolution. He bid successfully at the sale of Scott's Darien tracts and at the Charles Roberts sale of Quaker books.

In eleven years Winship had increased the size of the Library by one third. John Carter Brown collected widely. His son leaned toward high spots and polished the collection by replacing imperfect copies bought in a bibliographically less sophisticated era. Winship went back to the older pattern and interpreted "relating to America" in a most liberal fashion. But there were frustrations. In 1903 during the transition Henry Sotheran & Company of London offered him the fabled Sir Thomas Phillipps collection, suggesting that it might be possible to separate the Americana. Five years later the library of the great Latin American bibliographer, José Toribio Medina, was offered. The price was $50,000. That year the book funds totaled $10,000.

George Parker Winship's work extended beyond collecting to the need for making scarce research materials more readily available. The library published facsimile reprints of some of its rarer items. Then in 1912 it became the first library to purchase a Photostat machine, just a few months ahead of the New York Public Library. The next year the library offered for sale photo copies of a nearly complete set of the *Newport Mercury*, culled from the various files in Rhode Island. This, I believe, is one of the earliest examples of a large-scale use of photography to assist historians. Winship's other activities included the preparation of the first bibliography of Rhode Island imprints and the compilation of the first census of incunabula in American collections, a project continued by Miss Stillwell. He also led a survey of material for the history of printing in America sponsored by the Bibliographical Society of America.

By this time Winship had developed a style that one of his greatest fans described thus:

"THE LITERARY DEVICE of intentional double meaning is a familiar one, but the Winshipian style is not satisfied with that apparently simple game. If GPW is on the diamond, better look for a triple play — with no one safe at home."

An early example is a review in 1898. The book in question concerned the Zeno voyages to the North Atlantic, pre-Columbian and ever controversial. Winship was an authority on the subject. His second book, *Cabot Bibliography*, was then in preparation so he wrote of the author of the Zeno book:

"THE CERTAINTY AND CLEARNESS of his concluding summary, the generous fashion in which his theory is presented, the difficulty in discovering the precise grounds upon which the several steps of his argument are based, alike assure the acceptance of his ideal by those who will popularize his conclusions."

Throughout his years in Providence Winship never lost

contact with his old stamping grounds. He became a non-resident member of the Club of Odd Volumes in 1898 and a resident member in 1910. Archibald Cary Coolidge, Director of the Harvard University Library, was constantly passing along information about libraries and books in which Winship might be interested. Correspondence with William Coolidge Lane, Librarian of the Harvard College Library, and Alfred Potter, Assistant Librarian, was frequent. Correspondence with Hiram Bingham, pioneer Latin Americanist who is best known for his work at Machu Picchu in Peru, was extensive. Bingham was Honorary Curator of South American Literature and History at Harvard, and in 1905 Winship succeeded him.

Back in 1898 he had written to John Nicholas Brown about his membership in the COV:

"I NEED NOT ASSURE YOU of my personal interest in the club — which has already done much to supply a lack in Providence which I have felt personally, more and more with every occasion to compare the life and local spirit here with what I come in contact with whenever I go to Cambridge."

I would dearly love to see the letter which produced the following from Potter:

CAMBRIDGE, Mass. Feb. 1, 1910
"DEAR WINSHIP:

"Your levity and your gibes, Sir, are both ill-timed and misdirected. When a great institution is in the throes and agonies of an organic revolution, for an outsider and so-called friend of that institution to select that time for a base and atrociously unfair attack indicates on his part not merely a lack of loyalty and a deficiency but a diabolical delight in tormenting and harassing the officers of the said institution.

"But when the attack comes from one to whom has been given the honorary position of Curator, then although indeed he has never curated, the position becomes well-nigh insupportable. Such a grievance is not to be born without remonstrating and I therefore beg you to reconsider your hasty words!

"... But all will be forgiven if you will come and spend the night with me some time next week (any day after Monday).

YOURS SINCERELY"

Great things were beginning to happen at Harvard. Coolidge had taken over the leadership of the library and the Widener Memorial was only four years away.

Winship had made a place for himself in Providence which must have been strengthened when he married Clair Bliven in 1912. Their home was on Benevolent Street just around the corner from the JCB. On the other hand the tendency of Massachusetts Bay people, even those from the original Plymouth colony, to treat Rhode Islanders with some contempt was a practice of long standing. In any case on January 29th 1914 he wrote Henry N. Stevens as follows:

"To you, who live in nightly expectation of bombs, this will hardly be very exciting, but thereabouts I have succeeded in stirring up quite a bit of conversation. I have resigned.

"In May, my twentieth anniversary with the Library, I take over Livingston's position at Harvard, as Librarian of the Harry Widener collection. The position as it was first planned, would not have moved me, but Mrs. Widener decided she wanted me, and so I am going to try to make it a better place than this.

"It is modeled as nearly as may be on the place I have made in Providence. There was very little to choose between the two, except that in Providence the work is largely done, so far as laying down the lines for growth is concerned. The opportunities there are very great if I can make the most of them."

The Committee of Management accepted Winship's resignation and at the same meeting resolved:

"THAT INFORMAL ACTION of members of the Committee in inviting Champlin Burrage, Librarian of Manchester College, Oxford, to visit this country for the purpose of meeting the Committee, his expenses to be paid out of Library funds."

Mr. Burrage, a member of a family with Brown University connections, received his A. B. and M. A. from the University in 1896 and 1905. An A. B. D. from Newton Theological Seminary in 1905 and a Litt. B. from Oxford in 1909 followed.

At their meeting on April 6th 1914 the committee addressed a letter of appreciation, written by Mr. Kellen, to Mr. Winship, and then elected Mr. Burrage as his successor. All foresighted and efficient, one would think: not so.

The next day President Faunce, who was the Chairman of the Committee, wrote the following to Mr. Kellen, the Secretary of the Committee of Management:

"I SAW MISS STEERE [Winship's second in command] yesterday and found her hurt and indignant. According to her statement Mr. Burrage came to the library without introduction, and when asked for his name declined to give it, simply saying that he had been sent there by the Committee of Management to investigate the Library. He then proceeded to ask scores or hundreds of questions, to which the library staff submitted only because they believed an investigation had been ordered by our committee . . . I never knew that Mr. Burrage had been invited to come from Oxford until he actually appeared in Providence. I never knew that he had entered the library without introduction, and should have strongly objected had I known he was going there . . . I was thunder-struck yesterday afternoon when I learned that without authorization from our committee Mr. Burrage had cabled his resignation before we elected him . . ."

Out in California Mrs. John Nicholas Brown, a member of the Committee, was writing to Mr. Kellen:

"I HAVE AN EXTRAORDINARY TELEGRAM from Mr. Winship which was so vague in its wording that I hardly know what he means, stating that someone has suggested that his leaving the library meant wrecking the library and hopes that I will not give my consent to the plan. I do not know if he is referring to Mr. Burrage's election as librarian or not."

Kellen replied immediately:

"WHAT I HAD TO SAY about Winship in the 'letter' referred to him exclusively in his capacity as librarian; in all other respects I find and have found him 'impossible'. Mr. Winship had come to feel that he owned the Library and should dictate its policy after he had left to take charge of what he expects to be in a reasonable time a rival, if not an eclipsing collection. The truth is that he is going to Cambridge as a subordinate and a subordinate he will remain. So much for him. Unless all his intelligent sponsors are mistaken Mr. Burrage is fully qualified for the position."

Two years later the Committee of management abruptly fired Mr. Burrage.

George Parker Winship spent half of his career in Providence. He was forty-four years old when he went back to Harvard. Perhaps he was right when he said he had done all that he could in Providence. He had done a great deal. He started with a private library of extraordinary quality. He made it into a national institution. He was a man of broad vision and the imprint he left is still the strongest in the Library today. His advice was sought and followed by other collectors who wanted to establish their collections as independent libraries.

Everything I have ever heard in Providence about George Parker Winship has been expressed with affection. Exasperation, amusement, awe, irritation, and admiration are some of the other reactions I have encountered, but never resentment. When it came to being right his batting average was awfully good, and that is not always appreciated.

GPW in the Widener Memorial Room

He Cygnet Press will issue
shortly its first publication,
a reprint of the Life of St.
Jerome, in Italian, which is
found in few copies only of
the edition of his Letters printed at Ferrara
by Lorenzo de Rossi in 1497. It has apparently never since been reprinted. The little
woodcuts in the original edition are a-
mong the most typical and most charming of Italian book illustrations of the last
fifteenth century decade.

Prospectus for the first publication of the Cygnet Press, 1928

George Parker Winship:
Passionate Partisan of Fine Printing.

BY MARTIN W. HUTNER

President of the American Printing History Association.

In the heady early days of my flirtation with fine printing and
the world of books, which later led by happy degrees to a lifelong involvement, the name of George Parker Winship came
to my attention even before that of other, possibly more expected, names such as Bruce Rogers, A. S. W. Rosenbach, or
A. Edward Newton. Yet when Roger Stoddard suggested this
lecture to me, I realized that although I knew quite a bit
about Winship by this time, I also knew very little. The reason Winship was known to me so early on was that one
could not delve into matters concerning the Merrymount
Press without the name cropping up again and again. When I
say I knew much about Winship, I knew what I needed to
know about him, relevant to my collecting and personal research. But if I were to stand before this august audience, I
needed to know considerably more. First, I gathered up all
my personal Winshipiana. I was surprised to realize how extensive it was. All this had to be ingested anew. Then I
sought archival material relevant to Winship. I found and
visited three primary sources: the Huntington Library at San
Marino, the John Carter Brown Library at Providence, and
lastly, and hugely, here at Harvard.

When I say hugely, it is no overstatement. A dozen car-
tons hold Winship's scrupulously retained papers, ranging
from the beginning of the century to shortly before his death
at mid-century. In short, a professional lifetime of over fifty
years. I have spent many days over the last two years coming
back to this incredible resource which I commend as a rich
trove of not only George Parker Winship, but of scholarly
book, academic, library, and social history, and a good deal
more. There is a letter, for instance, from the poet Wallace
Stevens asking for a subscription to Winship's books; and another from the actress Dolores del Rio asking for background

information for a period movie she was about to make. I choose these two random, ephemeral letters to suggest that Winship's world and influence ultimately stretched far and wide. From this formidable mountain of information, I culled much material relevant to my particular subject — Winship and fine printing. Indeed, the subject of printing suffused the whole.

Although Winship, in fact, began life as a history major at Harvard, it wasn't long before he developed an interest, first in bibliography, and then in printing itself. Winship wrote: "Private Printing was all the rage at the time when I made the decision which cast my lot on the bookish side of a livelihood. Presses with queer names were sprouting at every crossroads, and clubs for book collectors camouflaged all sorts of publishing schemes . . . It was all very confusing to me, knowing nothing of the book trade then, for, as soon as I became a 'Private Librarian' I was appealed to for authoritative opinions and advice on every aspect of these always unique opportunities."[1]

Fortunately for him, Winship could turn almost immediately to another Rhode Islander, who was beginning his professional life just at the same time in the early eighteen-nineties, another of those now gone triune names, Daniel Berkeley Updike.

Winship continued: "Collecting was the newest fashion in the best circles; membership in the Grolier Club was one sure way of making a name on Wall Street . . . Clearly, there were not enough desirable books to go around. Above all, the demand outran the supply of books that the buyer and especially his friends, could recognize as proper possessions for a bibliophile. Private printing and limited editions went far to meet the need."[2]

Winship began his scholarly publishing in 1894 with a study of Coronado's journey to New Mexico, and just three years later — one hundred years ago — his first bibliographic work, entitled "Cabot Bibliography," was published. It appeared in the Providence Library's *Bulletin*.

In speaking of his employment as a private librarian to John Nicholas Brown, Winship was to say ". . . my own lot was cast in pleasanter places, with real books, and I escaped largely being drawn in the limited edition vortex."[3] He was soon to succumb to that vortex, but let it be said, with scholarship and grace. At first Winship acquired two early Elbert Hubbards and a bit of Strawberry Hill ephemera. Strange shelf-fellows one might say. "I lived," he wrote, "for some years with the Grolier Club books at hand; and William Morris's Kelmscotts were under a neighboring roof . . . The more I came to know about the market for choice books, the clearer it came to be that collecting is a factor that must be taken into account in any cultural future, and that there are not enough desirable books in the world to satisfy a demand . . . Inasmuch as my professional life was devoted to removing books from the possible future market, I came to have a feeling of obligation to replace the books which I supposed would never again get into circulation by others which might supply future collectors with something to talk about. Those unborn bibliophiles have been in the background of most of my printing ventures."[4]

Winship's printing ventures, at least his personal ones, were not to come until the early nineteen twenties, but it was his position as Brown librarian, and most particularly from 1904 when the library became an official part of the university, that his physical and professional proximity to Updike, gave him both example and standards. It must be said at this point, that whatever examples Winship had to hand, he must have been possessed of a good eye and excellent taste which developed early and quickly. Winship observed that from the experience of having his first Cabot bibliography reprinted by the Chiswick Press in 1900, "I learned a lot about bibliography and good printing during the year in which the book was in proof."[5] Soon Winship was to turn to other publishers and presses to print what was to become well over one hundred publications. Apart from a lifelong affinity and relationship with the Merrymount Press, Winship would employ for his own books virtually all of the Ivy League University presses in this country, as well as the Oxford, Palmer, Norwood, Southwood-Anthoensen, Lakeside, Pynson, Harbor, Chiswick, and Rudge presses, to name a few. He would also employ the design talents of Bruce Rogers, William Addison Dwiggins, and Rudolph Ruzicka among others. Before the end of the first decade of this century he turned to T. J. Cobden-Sanderson and his Doves Press to print his book on William Caxton.

While at the John Carter Brown Library, Winship was training his eye, not only by the constant acquisition of fine specimens of early printing, but by the necessity of turning out reports and library publications whose printing set a new standard for such publications. Many of these works were undertaken with the collaboration of the Merrymount Press which began with a volume devoted to the dedication of the John Carter Brown Library in 1903, issued in 1905. The connection between Updike, his press, and the library continued until Updike's death in 1941 and ended with the press's closing in 1949 under his partner John Bianchi. Updike was kin to the Brown family, and Harold Brown, a close childhood friend, was financially instrumental in enabling Updike to begin the Merrymount Press in 1893. Additionally, Updike was for many years a member of the John Carter Brown Library board. The reports of the corporation and routine library notes were part of the bread-and-butter of the Merrymount Press. But a number of grand facsimile publications for the library printed over the years by Merrymount insured the finest printing for the library. All of these publications had the particular and ongoing participation of Winship, chronicled in many letters to and from the press.

Perhaps the finest work Winship produced, and which Updike printed for the library, began in 1919: the multi-volume *Bibliotheca Americana Catalogue of the John Carter Brown Library*, published over a period of years. It is, arguably, one of the finest such catalogues ever produced; and typographically and aesthetically one of the most meticulous and handsome works to issue from the Merrymount Press. Certainly the sympathetic partnership, as it were, of Updike and Winship created this rare harmony.

But Winship was an exacting person, perhaps frequently adamantly so, and there exist a number of letters where Win-

DWIGGINS

A CHARACTERIZATION

BY

PAUL M. HOLLISTER

OF THE DESIGNER OF

THE MARK OF

THE CYGNET PRESS

CAMBRIDGE, MASSACHUSETTS

MDCCCCXXIX

Title- page of a Cygnet Press imprint designed by W. A. Dwiggins

WHEN WILLIAM CAXTON returned to London in the late autumn of 1476, he was about fifty-five years of age, a retired merchant who had for some years represented the commercial interests of the English traders at the principal continental town where their goods were bought & sold, a diplomat to whom had been entrusted the adjustment of treaty rights vitally affecting the English prestige and prosperity and who had more recently been attached to the court with which the English crown was most closely allied. Since his retirement from active business, he had devoted some of his time to literary effort, and he had travelled far enough to acquaint himself with the newest literary factor, a German invention of a mechanical substitute for manual labour, whereby the established method of reproducing individual copies of a book by hand writing was being supplanted by devices which produced machine made volumes in considerable numbers, each more or less identically like the others. ⁋ Born about the year 1422, Caxton began life, after a period of schooling, by being apprenticed in 1436 to one of the wealthiest and most successful of the London merchants of that day, a prominent member of the Mercers Company, who was chosen Lord Mayor of London for the year following that in which the young Caxton became a member of his household. The master and patron died in 1441, and

5

GPW, *William Caxton A Paper read at a meeting of the Club of Odd Volumes* (Hammersmith: Doves Press, 1909), first page of text

THE

JOHN CARTER BROWN
LIBRARY

A HISTORY

BY

GEORGE PARKER WINSHIP

PROVIDENCE
1914

Title-page of GPW's *History*,
designed and printed by D. B. Updike at the Merrymount Press

A potpourri of imprints from the Sign of the George
(Collection of Martin Hutner)

ship quite amazingly dictates technical typographic criticism to Updike. More surprisingly, Updike takes it.

Updike writes: "I agree with you that the red does not seem as good as the plain black from the title; and the Roman . . . I have changed to a lower case italic. You are quite right in saying that the prominent words were very often picked out in Roman."[6] And then in a letter of Winship to Updike several years later: "I do not care personally for so large an invitation — but that is no reason for not trying it this time — typographical experimentation being one reason for having you print our things." But then he goes on to say, "The weak spot seems to me the line in italic below the text — would it help to add the year . . . the shorter balances with the upper two lines."[7]

As early as 1906, there is a letter from Winship to Updike concerning a project in hand. "I fancy you will agree that less matter will look better on so small a page . . . would it not be well to put the Prefatory to the Reader either in small type, or in italics, so that it may not pretend to be as important . . . ?"[8]

There are numerous other projects where Winship very emphatically has his design and typographic say. One such book over which both men fretted was *James Browne, his writings in Prose and Verse*, of 1917. A number of years later, Stanley Morison, writing to Henry Lewis Bullen said, "About Winship, I am in correspondence with him [with respect to] the *Four Centuries [of Fine Printing]* . . . I am showing a title-page which he or Updike designed — I don't know which — but both claim it."[9]

Other examples of Winship's hands-on involvement with Merrymount printing are quite explicit. In a letter to Updike concerning a marked up proof for the John Carter Brown Library, "Report of the Committee of Management," Winship writes: "The top line is lonesome. 'Report' is either too small or too large . . . you may have some other suggestion to bring things to proportion."[10] And then again in another letter, "Isn't it leaning over backwards typographically to have less space between a period and the beginning of a new sentence than between other words in the same line?"[11]

There is no reply extant from Updike. But I suspect the superior and somewhat patronizing tone of the above criticism would leave Updike contemplating strangulation rather than punctuation. Interestingly and perhaps tellingly, the suggestions were not all one way. In an undated note to Winship, Updike writes: "I enclose herewith a page arranged as I should like to see it, and pulled on the paper that I should propose for it. It seemed to me that it would be rather nice if, in the margin here and there, notes were introduced in italic. Do you not think that would have rather a pretty and characteristic effect?"[12]

Would any of us have presumed to dictate, let alone suggest, typographic changes to Updike? Listen, in fact, to what John Bianchi wrote to Winship concerning his role as partner to Updike. Speaking of a book Bianchi had produced in Updike's absence: "He severely criticized it as he did everything he did not do himself. Everything was wrong with it — the type was too coarse, etc."[13] That Winship could do what he did — alter and specify typographic design to Updike, suggests that Updike, ultimately, must have held Winship in considerable respect. Their association parallels Winship's Brown and Harvard years, and beyond. Updike, in fact, was only eleven years older than Winship. And through these years, Winship, who admired Updike tremendously, became to a large extent Updike's Boswell, arranging exhibitions, writing articles and books, forming his own collection of and about the Merrymount Press. Toward the end of his life, Winship wrote a major book on Updike and the Press, which expanded and enlarged an earlier essay which had been printed in Vienna in the nineteen twenties.[14] I suggest that this early and lifelong association with Updike proved to be one of the major forces in the formation of Winship's taste and typographic distinction. Certainly there were other printers. Winship had a great interest in William Addison Dwiggins, Bruce Rogers, and Rudolph Ruzicka, as indicated earlier, and he did not hesitate to use their example, and to employ them from time to time in his public and private printing.

Winship corresponded with virtually all of the major printers of his time, having no hesitation in either employing or criticizing them. Carl Purington Rollins, for one, writes to Winship, "I think your criticism of the placing of the type on the cover . . . is justified."[15]

Frederic Warde sent proofs of a typeface he was working on in 1925 for Winship's approval. "I [am] happy to know that you approved the new type. I am having the ascending l.c. [lower case] characters recut, and also the roman l.c. and hope to combine the two founts in the usual manner in book work."[16]

Winship had a great interest in Bruce Rogers whom he was always thinking of using for his projects, and there are many letters from Rogers to Winship. Either Rogers is too busy, or going abroad, or one thing or another keep him from working on the project of the moment. His letters to Winship are admiring and friendly and the two send books as presents to each other. There is a very interesting letter of Winship's to a publisher wherein he discusses Updike and Rogers. Winship comments on two of the greatest forces of printing in America in the first half of this century; and it is, in its candid estimation, an important, and highly perceptive document.

"I STAND BY MY OPINION that Updike is the greatest book maker of all time and I'm equally of opinion that Rogers is equally entitled to be called the greatest printer of our day. I stop there because we cannot be sure of some things about Geoffrey Tory and curiously the things we are not sure of are about the same as those that I'm not sure the future will say about Rogers which supports Alfred Pollard's characterization of Rogers as the reincarnation of Tory.

"This explains my saying that Updike was not a printer. No more was Rogers, as a livelihood, but worked closer to type and press and paper than Updike ever got . . .

"I claim nothing for Updike that raises any comparison with Rogers. The distinction as I see it is that Updike throughout printed books that would have been printed anyhow, but better than they would have been done anywhere else. Rogers was almost always engaged upon things that would not have been done if he had not done them. . . . [If he had been] employed as a portrait painter or a silver worker [then he] would have been engaged to do a specific job, because he had a unique genius, a brilliant imagination, and execution, unmatched, if ever, since Tory.

"The minor half of Updike's output ought to be mentioned — the multitudinous pieces of job work which are as much ahead of all job work (except Rogers) as Updike books surpass other publications. But Updike's invitations and notices and suchlike, which have all his taste and dignity and a great deal of imagination and almost humor, just have not got the bubbling genius that is Bruce Rogers."[17]

Winship could demolish as readily as praise printers, as in this single sentence about John Henry Nash in a letter to Horace Hart. "Did I tell you that someday I want to find a Californian to do John Henry Nash? The illustrations would be the most god-awful printing ever perpetrated in the USA."[18]

But unlike Updike or even Rogers, who weren't keen on actual printing, Winship had by mid-life an urge, perhaps unconscious, to actually print for himself. This opportunity presented itself when George Parker Winship, Jr., aged six, was given a little printing press by a family friend in 1920. This was promptly and appropriately named, "The Sign of the George." The first item which father and son produced was entitled *How the Monkey Got Its Tail*. This press debut is illustrated with five small cuts, runs to twelve pages, and is handsewn in various art and paste paper wrappers. George Jr., in a letter to the author, wrote: "GPW was in 1920 becoming a rare-book man and teaching about Gutenberg and Plantin and so on. His old friend and housemate Walter Ball [who gave the press] might have thought, 'What does George know? Had he ever had printer's ink under his finger nails?' . . . I can recall my dad seated with the printer's stick in his hand, the type case propped on an armchair before him."[19]

A fair number of items were made under the "George" press imprint and were cited by Will Ransom in his *Private Presses and Their Books* of 1929. Ransom writes, "No Press could operate in greater privacy and freedom than the Sign of the George, maintained by George Parker Winships, I and II. Mr. Winship says: 'The thing has been a plaything from the start and I've refused to spoil it for myself by allowing it to be formalized. If the press has any policy, it has been to print things of literary interest — but of no importance.' "[20]

Ransom lists ten major works and a few minor. (This isn't a strictly accurate account as there were other items printed during this period but unlisted.) Ransom further notes that "all the work is set by hand in Monotype Caslon, and no statement is ever made of the number of copies printed."

The question of edition limitation is an interesting aside with respect to Winship. He was frequently adamant about overruns, but clearly had a double standard. Either he made no mention of limitation for his own press production or he was vague, such as "Two Hundred copies more or less." But he could be a martinet about copies with others. He once had Updike against the wall, desperately defending his need for overage. What was good for the goose was clearly not for the cygnet, as he was still fulminating about overruns even in the late nineteen forties.

Ransom, who recorded nearly a decade of work at Winship's home press, the Sign of the George, also cites the then newly-founded Cygnet Press, begun in 1928, listing only the first work of the press, *Vita de Sancto Hieronymo*, published that year. This small book of thirty-six pages is handsomely printed on handmade paper. It is a charming work containing reproductions of a series of Italian Renaissance woodcuts, and it is printed in Italian Old Style. This first *incunabulum* of the Cygnet press was printed by the Harbor Press. Ransom states that the proprietors were "a group of bookish enthusiasts, chief among them being Mr. George Parker Winship."[21] The other "bookish enthusiasts" were in fact one man — Philip Hofer — whose subsequent multitudinous enthusiasms and accomplishments might fairly allow him to be referred to in the plural. No doubt Ransom was alluding to the select student composition of Winship's class, Fine Arts 5e, of which Hofer had been a member. In any event the association between Winship and Hofer was significant, long-standing, and far-reaching. And though the Cygnet Press was to be a sometime thing, the quality of each work produced in subsequent years and the amount of time and effort each man expended is evidence of their enthusiasm, knowledge, taste, and skill. Fine Arts 5e, The History of the Book, was started by Winship at Harvard and met once a week at Widener. It was limited to the number of students who could comfortably fit around the table in the center of the room. Winship handpicked his students. It must have been gratifying for him that so many of them went on to become distinguished book collectors, curators, writers, and scholars. A short list of his students reads like a book-world *Who's Who*. Besides Philip Hofer, Carl Pforzheimer, Lucius Beebe, David Randall, Boies Penrose, Reginald Allen, George Harding, Stanley Marcus, Walter Muir Whitehill, Emerson Wulling, and Horace Hart, were among the elect. It is interesting that a number of future book studies had their genesis in the course. Horace Hart's *Bibliotheca Typographica* of 1933, which boasted a preface by Winship, had begun as a student project.[22] Indeed, despite the fact that the book is a mature work, Winship's introduction has a whiff of pedagogical censure — praising with faint damning. This mixture of frankness and implied criticism is a constant and typical feature of Winship's writing and correspondence. Winship carried on a correspondence with many of his students until his death in 1952. Many of these students became mature colleagues as the years passed. Apparently none of them lost either appreciation or enthusiasm (which in some cases amounted to awe) for their former teacher.

It was with Philip Hofer, perhaps more than anyone since Updike, that Winship in middle and late life had the most fruitful relationship. The Cygnet Press, though a part-time undertaking, became for both Hofer and Winship an outlet for their fine printing urges. The charming *Tantalus,* which was printed in 1937, contained a superb woodcut by Rudolph Ruzicka of a Holbein drawing belonging to Hofer. The correspondence, sometimes conducted on two continents between the two men, exhibits the intellectual and aesthetic interests of both, their love of fine printing, and their passion for bookmaking. Back and forth the letters fly, full of talk of paper, ink, typography, proofing, publishing, and distribution. This is a microcosm of the world both men loved, explored, and enlarged in their separate and collective ways. After a time, as Hofer grew older and "Dear Mr. Winship" turned into "Dear George," Hofer asserted himself more and more; and the design of Cygnet publications clearly becomes very much a shared project. Whatever maturity *cum* familiarity came with advancing years, Hofer would use the word "anxious" whenever he did anything without first consulting Winship.

One of the letters from Winship in 1937, concerning the preparation of the *Tantalus,* is a particularly good example of the care, historical perspective, scholarship, and aesthetic sensibility — as well as temperament — that informed and infused his work. The letter, quoted in full, concerns the search for an appropriate Greek type to use in the text:

"DEAR PHIL,

"I'm feeling better, thank you.

"Fobes reports that he sees nothing wrong with the Greek, except for a couple of broken letters, except in line 4 of Pindar the 14th letter, a, should be a. But to prove my broad-mindedness, this seems to me hardly worth bothering about, just to preserve our scholarship. Also, of course, he notes that Pindar should begin with a capital letter.

"I never doubted that this Greek type is all that the Harbor press knows how to get. When I see Rogers, I'll ask where Rudge got the type used in *Champfleury.* And as to worrying about time, I'm guessing that the Clarendon would have beaten Linotype in time.

"My quarrel is that we are perpetuating a crime committed by Aldus Manutius in the year 1500, when he made a commercial success of a mongrel bastard script letter which none of the men you mention nor anyone else knew about the actual Hellenistic scribal practice to object to, until Robert Proctor, working at another problem, realized that it was all wrong for Greek bookmaking.

"I do not object to run-over lines, but I see no reason why you and I should accept and pay for laziness, ignorance, and stupidity trying to pass itself off as diletante [sic] typography — Oh, Damn, I'm not feeling as much better as I thought.

"It isn't that I have the slightest anxiety that this will not be a very sweet and pleasing setting forth of the Holbein-Ruzicka picture, but that it seems to me that it might have been better, within the specified limitations.

"Sorry to be so persnickety."[23]

Thus we see how first the historian scholar, then the private and public librarian, with an eye and a passion for fine book design and typography, develops into the legendary teacher, gadfly, and printing enthusiast. Winship wrote or edited well over a hundred books, articles, and essays. As the years progressed the lion's share of his writing became either bibliographical or book-arts oriented. Winship's earliest writing concerns his initial and lifelong primary interest in early Latin American and North American colonial bibliography. But by the middle nineteen twenties, the subject of printing per se accelerates to the extent that well over three-quarters of his writing concerns printing and presses. If we eliminate articles and books concerning literature, history, or bibliography, then Winship's entire bibliography contains roughly one third devoted exclusively to fine press printing. Additionally, there were the products of his two private printing ventures. Besides writing about Caxton, Winship wrote on Gutenberg and Aldus with as much authority and passion as he did on contemporary printing.

Randolph G. Adams, discovered early in life by Winship in a chance encounter, and recommended immediately by him to head the William L. Clements Library, wrote of Winship toward the end of Winship's life: "George Parker Winship is a conscious New England Puritan of the John Winthrop type to which are added the characteristics of a Machiavelli brought up in Johann Gutenberg's printing shop . . . Owl-eyed professional scholars who sniff at rare books as 'unimportant' irk George Parker Winship and he often confounds and confuses them with his calm statement, 'No it's not important —

it's just nice.' Similarly, it was George Parker Winship who outraged humorless librarians by saying 'These books are not meant to be read; they are meant to be collected'."[24]

Recognized during his lifetime as a scholar-librarian who valued and loved the book itself as deeply as its contents, George Parker Winship required the hundreds of books emanating either from his pen or those books, pamphlets, and ephemera over which he had control, to possess in the printing and production the highest quality he could summon. It was appropriate that the Society of Printers, on the occasion of their thirty-fifth anniversary, chose to offer Winship honorary membership, in Updike's apt phrase "as a fit occasion for celebrating some of those who were doing the most for American printing."[25]

It was Stanley Morison who, in a letter to Updike, with a touch of archness perhaps, but in appropriately classical terms, summed up Winship best: "Mr. G. P. Winship *clarum et venerabile nomen*."[26] Illustrious and distinguished name. And so he was.

Fine Arts 5e:
The Invention and the Aftermath.

BY MICHAEL B. WINSHIP

Professor of English at University of Texas, Austin.

When George Parker Winship turned forty on 29 July 1911, he was firmly established in a successful career at the John Carter Brown Library. Before the end of his fortieth year, he married Claire Bliven of Westerly, Rhode Island, fifteen years his junior: George Parker Winship Jr., his first child, was born in March 1914. But if Winship expected to remain settled in Providence to raise his new family and finish his career, it was not to be. In 1915 he moved his family to Cambridge to take up a new career at the Harvard College Library.

A few years later, in his twenty-fifth Harvard class report, Winship elaborated on his recent appointment as Librarian of the Harry Elkins Widener Collection:

"Since May 1, 1915, when I took charge of my new job, I have been trying to solve the interesting problem of making a somewhat ornamental fifth wheel carry its share of the load in an institution which is not accustomed to such luxuries. . . . The Harvard Library has been, in the opinion of many who use it, the best students' library in the world. It is also a very great collection of rare and valuable books, which have never had the care and attention that they deserve. If this can now be given to them, and an increasing number of owners of precious volumes realize that their treasures will be appreciated, intelligently preserved for the delight of future booklovers, and made available under proper restrictions and oversight for the use of investigators, the Harvard Library can confidently anticipate rivalling some day even the Bodleian at Oxford. Laying the foundations for such a future is what my present job calls for."[1]

An ambitious program, certainly, and this afternoon I want to look at one important way he set about achieving it. Through his course, Fine Arts 5e, Winship trained a generation of Harvard students to love and appreciate books — as collectors and donors — and Harvard and its libraries have harvested the fruits ever since.

Winship was not the first choice for, nor the first appointed to, the position of Librarian of the Harry Elkins Widener Collection. This was the creation of a member of the Harvard Class of 1907, who decided that it should be given to Harvard after his death, whenever the College should have a suitable building in which to receive it. After Harry Elkins Widener died at twenty-seven with the sinking of the Titanic, that condition was generously fulfilled by his mother, Mrs. George D. Widener, who funded not just memorial rooms, but also the new Widener Library building.[2] Mrs. Widener first selected Dr. Luther S. Livingston, a distinguished bibliographer, cataloger, and book dealer, who had guided young Harry Widener in his bookbuying, to oversee her son's collection in its new home as the centerpiece of the new college library building, but Livingston did not survive to take up the post. He and his wife, the former Flora V. Milner, moved to Cambridge in 1914, but he was already severely ill with a crippling disease (I am not sure exactly what). Despite hope of recovery, he died on Christmas Eve 1914, before the new library building and rooms were completed.[3]

I also do not know who put Winship forward as a candidate to fill the vacancy, but it happened quickly. He had friends, certainly, both in Cambridge and elsewhere, and I can only imagine that discussion had already taken place behind the scenes. On 8 January 1915 Winship received a telegram from Belle da Costa Greene, J. P. Morgan's indomitable librarian:

"JUST HAD A VERY LONG TALK WITH MRS WIDENER POSITION IS YOUR[S] IF YOU WANT IT HOPE YOU WILL CONSIDER ADVANTAGES TO GO[ING] IN ACCEPTING LET ME HEAR IF POSSIBLE"[4]

That same day Flora Livingston made clear in a letter to Winship that she had expected herself to be named curator in place of her husband, but that she now accepts that she will not be—indeed she claims to have just realized that it will be Winship who is named.[5] On 10 January 1915, Winship wrote to Mrs. Widener in regard to salary,[6] and five days later Archibald Cary Coolidge, Director of the University Libraries, reports to Winship that "The President tells me that things are now definitely settled, and that you are coming here."[7] The appointment was presented to the Harvard Corporation for vote on 25 January 1915, and announced publicly in the *Boston Transcript* on 27 January 1915. Winship took up his new duties 1 May 1915, with Flora Livingston named his assistant: their first order of business was the installation of the Widener books in the new library in preparation for the Widener building's dedication on Commencement Day, 24 June 1915.[8]

Of Winship's qualifications for his new position and of his proven record of accomplishment over twenty years at the John Carter Brown Library, Tom Adams informs us. An exchange of letters between Winship and Coolidge indicates that from the beginning he had a plan for achieving his goal of making rare books a central and vital part of the Harvard College Library.

Let me elaborate. From 1910 to 1912 the Harvard College Librarian, William Coolidge Lane, had given a course on the history of printing, "designed primarily for members of the Graduate School of Business Administration who were preparing to take up publishing as their professional occupation."[9] This course, Fine Arts 5e, Winship was charged to take over, and while he did request the literature describing Lane's course from Coolidge, he clearly had a different audience and different purpose in mind. In a letter of 24 January 1915 he explained:

"As to the Course on "The Printed Book"—the confirmation troubles me less than the standing of the course. . . . A graduate course is altogether to my liking, if it counts for some degree, and if there is some chance of a nucleus of students. It ought, I think, to be open to Seniors—Juniors by special arrangement—partly because I count on this to interest Mrs. Widener. My idea would be to try to troll into it some of the undergraduates who have begun to buy books — and make the Widener fireplace a meeting place where new purchases will be looked over — & many possibilities considered. . . . I have been planning such a course at Brown — for years — so it is not a new scheme. I feel quite confident that a certain amount of work can be provided for the students — so that it need not be altogether a snap course. . . ."[10]

In February Coolidge reported that "The Fine Arts Department and the Business School are anxious to make some announcement soon about a course in the 'History of the Book' for next year," but Winship responded that he had already, at the "earnest solicitation of the Chairman of the Fine Arts Department," prepared an extended description for the department circular.[11] "The bait is fairly obvious — & may be too much sugared," he continued, but judge for yourselves:

"THIS COURSE IS INTENDED for men who are interested in books as objects of art, and who desire to possess or to produce beautiful books. The lectures on the history of printing and its subsidiary crafts will be supplemented by discussions of the characteristic qualities which affect the excellence and value of any volume. The physical make-up of a book and the conditions governing its manufacture will be explained with sufficient detail to provide a basis for sound judgment of the quality of any piece of work.

"The lectures will treat of book production from the period of the illuminated manuscripts to the present time. The work of the men who made noteworthy contributions to the advancement or the deterioration of the art of fine book-making will be studied historically and technically. Considerable attention will be given to the presses which are now producing good work.

"The incidental aspects of the subject which affect the collecting of books will be considered. An important object of the course is to train the taste of book-buyers, and to cultivate a well-informed judgment of the value of rare and attractive volumes. The methods by which books of moderate importance are made to seem desirable will be explained. Old and modern examples of good and bad book-making will be shown. There will be opportunities to examine volumes belonging to members of the class and to express opinions as to their fundamental and commercial value."[12]

Lane, for one, thought this description "capital and most attractive," likely to attract at least ten, and possibly as many as twenty-five, applicants. He added, however: "I hope you will also keep in mind, as I tried to do, the needs of the prospective publisher."[13] Despite this appeal, Winship's aim was not prospective professionals, but rather those who would make the study and collecting of books a life-long avocation. This he saw as central to his vision. Subsequently, on 10 April 1915, Winship was appointed Lecturer on the History of Printing, and the following fall he offered his course, Fine Arts 5e ("The History of the Printed Book"), for the first time. As long as he remained active at Harvard, he offered the course every year, save 1926–27, and with considerable success.[14] A list of some of his students illustrates his achievement:

HARRY CROSBY, poet, sunworshipper, and with his wife Caresse proprietor of the Black Sun Press;

DAVID P. WHEATLAND, whose superb collection of books on electricity is now in the Houghton Library;

GEORGE T. GOODSPEED, who took up his father's role as quintessential yankee bookseller;

DOUGLAS H. GORDON, whose magnificent collection of French literature is now in Charlottesville, much to the delight and edification of present-day students at Terry Belanger's Rare Book School;

STANLEY MARCUS of Dallas, founder of the Book Club of Texas and collector of, among other things, Christmas and miniature books;

BOIES PENROSE of Philadelphia, famous as a collector of English travel books and manuscripts;

WALTER MUIR WHITEHILL, antiquarian, local historian, and worthy librarian of the Boston Athenæum;

CARL H. PFORZHEIMER JR., who formed the collection

documenting Shelley and his circle now at the New York Public Library;

ARTHUR A. HOUGHTON JR., collector of Keats books and generous donor of the Houghton Library building;

PHILIP HOFER, later curator and generous mainstay of Harvard's collections of printing and graphic arts.

An impressive list, and there are many more — Alfred Reginald Allen, Lucius Beebe, Daniel Bianchi, Horace Hart, Lincoln Kirstein, Beaumont Newhall — bookmen and bibliophiles all![15]

Just how did Winship nurture a love of books and collecting in his students so effectively? Fortunately several students have left reminiscences of the course that describe his approach.[16] Boies Penrose's account is particularly evocative:

"... IT WAS NO ORDINARY COURSE, to be enrolled in simply by filling in a form at the beginning of term. Admission was rigorously guarded by the master himself, who, in all deference, was considerable of a snob, and who always wanted to be sure that his students were properly qualified (sic). In consequence 5e became known as one of the more exclusive clubs of Harvard . . .

"Not only did the standards of admission mark it off from other courses; its physical setting was likewise unique — the Widener Room, that superb book-lined *prunkzimmer,* with easy chairs and an open fire, and all the sybaritic comforts of a palace. This was indeed the environment that Winship loved: the environment of a connoisseur. . . .

"We would sit around a long table very informally. At the head of the table reclined Winship, a short, wiry man, with strong glasses and a spade beard . . . intermittently handing around illuminated manuscripts and incunabula for our inspection. Technical instruction was at a minimum; aesthetic appreciation and cultural background at a maximum. It was the book as creation, as a work of art, as an important factor in its time and place, that he stressed, rather than the devitalizing details of pagination and collation. And he stressed these things very well; so well, in truth, that most of us were carried away with enthusiasm. His lectures were perhaps dis-

proportionately devoted to the fifteenth-century: we had two
or three at the start given over to the manuscript tradition
behind printing; then the bulk of the course allotted to incunabula. The sixteenth century was polished off in a single
lecture; the seventeenth never mentioned at all; the eigh-
teenth got three afternoons, and the presses of the late nine-
teenth and early twentieth centuries were given a parting
salute at the end of the course. That was his method and he
stuck to it. We usually had a very excellent tea served in the
Widener Room after the lectures, and we could stay on till
the place was locked up, looking at Harry Widener's rarities.
No wonder that most of us finished with the conviction that
Winship was a great teacher, who had made a profound mark
on our cultural background."[17]

Surviving documents confirm this account. Admission was by
permission of the instructor, and Winship is reported to have
told his successor, William A. Jackson, in typically provoca-
tive fashion that he selected students by "Whiskey breath and
club pin."[18] Letters of application to the course substantiate
this, as for example one from Thomas M. Torrey that reports
"Both here at the Phoenix and at the Hasty Pudding I have
heard reports that Fine Arts 5E escapes the blemish of other
supposedly 'easy' courses, dullness. Such an offer, you must
admit, is tantalizing."[19]

Grading was indeed flexible. Walter Whitehill explains:

"THE STANDARD GRADE was a gentleman's C, which was
quite automatically bestowed unless the student showed co-
gent cause why he needed something else. If a gentleman
firmly wished, for his own reasons, to flunk out of Harvard
College and needed an E to accomplish this, Winship would
oblige."[20]

Winship's emphasis on early printing is confirmed by his
short study *From Gutenberg to Plantin: An Outline of the Early
History of Printing* (1926). This work was later expanded as
the Rosenbach lectures and published as *Printing in the Fifteenth Century* (1940), a volume dedicated to "F A 5e And to a

few score Harvard College students whose attendance at the meetings of that Fine Arts course on the History of the Printed Book between 1915 and 1931 contributed largely to formulating some of the opinions set forth in these lectures."[21] These two publications also indicate that Winship's focus was on the cultural and social history of printing — what we might call the history of the book — rather than on the technical details of bibliography. A list of recommended reading for 1931–32 includes among "Important Reading" both his own *From Gutenberg to Plantin* and R. B. McKerrow's *Introduction to Bibliography*, but students are advised to read only enough of each chapter of the latter "to get an idea of what the book is about."[22]

Also included here among "Important Reading" were A. W. Pollard's *Fine Books* and Will Ransom's *Private Presses and their Books*, indications that fine printing was a second major focus of Winship's course. Listed as "Useful Reading" were accounts of the work of John Baskerville, Horace Walpole, William Pickering, William Morris, Daniel Berkeley Updike, and Bruce Rogers.[23]

The examinations in the course also reflected Winship's distinctive approach. Here are some of his questions:

"How did the men who have been discussed in this course influence their contemporaries?" (1916)

"Describe the six books examined in connection with this course which you would most like to have in your library?" (1916)

"What is Bibliography? In what ways would you expect it to prove helpful in work in other fields of study?" (1930)

"Write a characterization of three or more bookmen, dealers, collectors, or bibliographers, with whom you are acquainted personally or about whom you have read or heard. *Please omit any reference to the one whom you have probably seen most regularly since College opened this autumn.*" (1931)

The structure of Winship's examinations was also flexible: some questions were noted as optional or less important, and once Winship advised students that "A thoughtful answer to any one question will count for more than shorter answers to all, but please keep to the subject under discussion." (1925)[24] Winship emphasized and encouraged his students' own interests and collecting activities. After Maurice Firuski, with Winship's encouragement, opened the Dunster House Bookshop in Cambridge in 1919, this establishment became a near-at-hand resource for Winship's teaching.[25] In 1922 a former student of Fine Arts 5e, Gustave Pabst, established a prize for the student who had "accomplished most" in the class: $50 for a book "in which he may be especially interested" given with the "honest hope that others may find the course . . . the beginning of a life-long interest."[26]

As part of the course, students were required "to prepare a written report upon the bibliography of some subject of especial interest,"[27] and many chose to investigate books in their own possession, often comparing them to copies at Harvard or in local bookstores. The student reports that I have been able to examine show a remarkable range and sophistication. They include:

Paul Henle's "Bibliographical Report on Hobbes' 'Leviathan'," based on two Harvard copies and one in the Dunster Bookshop.

Julius Birge's on "William Keeney Bixby: Octopus of Book-Collectors," inspired by eight books from Bixby's collection that had been left him in his grandfather's will.

Alexander Duncan Langmuir's ". . . Some Old and Interesting Facts Concerning the Boston Editions of the *Tribune Primer A Little Book of Nonsense* by Eugene Field," reporting on multiple copies he examined in the Boston bookstores.

Holland Bennett's "Bibliography of Twenty-Four Elzevir 'Republics' and General Observations Based on the Bibliography together with A Short History of the Elzevirs as Publishers" accounting twenty-four Elzevirs of his own and about [sic] fifteen Harvard copies.

And, finally, Eugene Du Bois's "Two Maps of the Gold Regions of California in 1849 A Bibliography." It describes three copies, one in his own possession, and is dedicated "to the man who has made that course the most interesting one at Harvard."[28]

Clearly Winship successfully inspired and convinced many of his students of the importance of books. Upon graduation, one former student, L. Cabot Briggs, wrote to Winship on 26 June 1931 in appreciation: "I want to tell you how much I have enjoyed knowing you, both personally, and as a teacher of one of the few remaining courses of the sort that went to make up the once famous Harvard liberal education which seems of late to have gone rather out of fashion."[29]

If I have emphasized Winship's teaching this afternoon, I do not mean to slight his other activities and contributions during his Harvard College Library career. Within the library, he helped organize the College's special collections in the Treasure Room, where he took charge as Assistant Librarian in the College Library in 1926 after his removal from the Widener Collection as a result of increasing friction with Mrs. Rice, the former Mrs. Widener.[30] In this new position he became directly involved in library development, both raising money and attracting collections, to support the Library (a response — at least in part — to similar activities by Chauncey Brewster Tinker at Yale). From 1920 he edited the *Harvard Library Notes* to report on library matters of interest to the Harvard community. He also continued to be a productive historical and bibliographical scholar, among many other things by his service in the preparation of the Bibliographical Society of America's *Census of Fifteenth Century Books Owned in America* (1919). As Martin Hutner describes, he was an active supporter of American fine printing. After he moved with his family to a farm in Charles River in 1919, he established his own private press, "The Sign of the George," where he produced a number of whimsical items including first editions of Stevenson, Kipling, and Henry James.[31] And throughout he maintained an active social life, participating in and addressing the numerous scholarly and social organizations of which he was a member. All these too deserve to be chronicled, but that would take another talk.

One of his activities of these years merits more than passing mention, for it is closely allied with his teaching. In 1927 he established the John Barnard Associates, an organization that honored the goals of its namesake, an eighteenth-century Massachusetts minister who (as Winship quaintly declared) "loved books and did what he could for Harvard."[32] Made up primarily of current and former students from Fine Arts 5e, the Associates enjoyed exhibitions, dinners at the Club of Odd Volumes, and trips over Christmas vacation to New York City to call on such bookish establishments as the Grolier Club, the American Typefounders Foundation Library and Museum, and the bookshops of E. H. Wells and Dr. A. S. W. Rosenbach. A number of burlesque and ephemeral accounts of these occasions were printed: they clearly indicate that members partook of liquid as well as bookish stimulation as part of the experience.[33] More seriously, the Associates also sponsored occasional publications: the 1927 club book, printed in 160 copies only, is itself a collector's rarity as a production of Bruce Rogers and was followed in 1928 by *A Leaf of Grass from Shady Hill,* which prints a poem in imitation of Whitman's *Leaves of Grass* and a review of that work's first edition, both written by Charles Eliot Norton. In 1929 the Associates produced a facsimile of Harvard's *Shelley Notebook* with notes and postscript by George Edward Woodberry. A fourth and final publication, a sampler with autobiographical notes from Walter Crane's *Hazelford Sketch Book* appeared in 1937, although other activities seemed to have ceased in 1933. In one real sense, though, the Barnard Associates continue today, for in 1968 former members established a fund for "a series of lectures on appropriate topics, to be sponsored by the Houghton Library and entitled the George Parker Winship Lectures."[34] This booklet prints the sixty-fifth through sixty-seventh in that series.

Early in 1932 Winship fell ill with what was eventually diagnosed as pernicious anemia, and Harvard granted him medical leave. Although he survived twenty years and continued scholarly work for more than ten, his active service as teacher and librarian was for all intents and purposes over. On 15 June 1932 Kenneth B. Murdock, who himself had been a student in Fine Arts 5e the first year that Winship offered it, wrote from the Office of the Dean that Winship's appointment as Lecturer on the History of Printing had not been renewed. He explained:

"FINE ARTS 5E does not seem at the present time to be an indispensable course and there has been some doubt in the minds of the Fine Arts Department as to whether it should be continued. There have also been some complaints about the grading in the course, and all things considered it seems better not to attempt to continue it . . ."[35]

In Winship's absence, Mrs. Helen Betts Allen was named to act in charge of the Treasure Room. Winship formally retired in 1937, and soon after William A. Jackson was named his successor.[36] On 24 January 1938, in a birthday letter to his son Stephen, my father, Winship commented on the appointment in generous fashion: "Bill Jackson . . . is far and away the best man for the job in this country — the only person whom I regard as in every way an improvement on his predecessor. . . . Nobody else would have given confidence in the Harvard Library, to the bookcollecting crowd."[37] Jackson in turn is said to have felt that "Winship lacked something in the academic approach to bibliography," but also to have recognized his predecessor's accomplishment: "It seems to me that anytime I approach people about a gift toward the purchase of a rare book for the collection, the most generous turn out to be old students of Professor Winship."[38]

In 1925 George H. Sargent wrote an article for *The Publishers' Weekly* entitled "Making the New Book Collectors." He describes at length and with approval Winship's Fine Arts 5e course, stating that it "has done more than any one thing, I think, toward making the Harvard book collectors of the future."[39] For my part, I hope that I have convinced you of the truth of his observation, and as one who also aims to teach my own students to understand and appreciate the value of the books, manuscripts, and other materials that document human history and accomplishment, I can only marvel at his success. If the essential role of the special collections librarian is to collect, preserve, and make such materials available, then Winship's special genius as a Harvard College librarian was to show how those goals can be accomplished within the university environment by teaching students to understand and treasure, support and participate in those important activities.

Notes

I would like to thank Roger Stoddard, the Houghton Library, Harvard; Norman Fiering, the John Carter Brown Library, Brown University; Sara S. Hodson, the Henry E. Huntington Library; Virginia Smyers, the Houghton Library; and Harley Holden, Harvard University Archives, for their kind assistance and for permission to quote from material in their institutions. Thanks, too, to Michael Winship and George Parker Winship, Jr., for their thoughtful advice and information.

1. George Parker Winship, "Recollections of a Private Printer," *The Colophon*, n.s. III, 2 (1938), p. 210.

2. Ibid, p. 210 f.

3. Ibid, p. 211.

4. Ibid, p. 211.

5. Ibid, p. 212.

6. TLS, Daniel Berkeley Updike to G. P. Winship, 27 December 1910, John Carter Brown Library.

7. ALS, G. P. Winship to D. B. Updike, 7 February 1915, John Carter Brown Library.

8. TLS, G. P. Winship to D. B. Updike, 1 November 1906, Huntington Library.

9. Stanley Morison to Henry Bullen, 28 April 1924, Columbia University Library.

10. G. P. Winship, Notations on Proof, 11 June 1912, Huntington Library.

11. ALS, G. P. Winship to D. B. Updike, 8 October 1914, Huntington Library.

12. ANS, D. B. Updike to G. P. Winship, [N. D.], Harvard University Archives.

13. TLS, John Bianchi to G. P. Winship, 22 March 1946, Harvard University Archives.

14. G. P. Winship, *The Merrymount Press of Boston: An Account of the Work of Daniel Berkeley Updike* (Vienna: Herbert Reichner, 1929) and *Daniel Berkeley Updike and the Merrymount Press* (Rochester: The Printing House of Leo Hart, 1947).

15. TLS, Carl P. Rollins to G. P. Winship, 31 December 1917, Harvard University Archives.

16. ALS, Frederic Warde to G. P. Winship, 11 December 1925, Harvard University Archives.

17. TLS, G. P. Winship to "Dear Brooks," 14 June 1942, Harvard University Archives.

18. TLS, G. P. Winship to Horace Hart, 31 December 1944, Harvard University Archives.

19. TLS, George Parker Winship, Jr., to Martin Hutner, 1 February 1997.
20. Will Ransom, *Private Presses and Their Books* (New York: R. R. Bowker Company, 1929), p. 117 f.
21. Ibid, p. 241.
22. Horace Hart, *Bibliotheca Typographica . . . with an introduction by George Parker Winship* (Rochester: The Printing House of Leo Hart, MCMXXXIII).
23. TLS, G. P. Winship to Philip Hofer, 10 June 1937, Harvard University Archives.
24. Randolph Adams, *The Quarto*, The University of Michigan, no. 11 (April 1946), p. 2.
25. Charles A. Rheault, Jr., *SP at 75: The Society of Printers, 1955–1980* (Boston: the Society, 1981), p. 10.
26. Stanley Morison to D. B. Updike, 9 March 1924, in *Stanley Morison & D. B. Updike: Selected Correspondence*, edited by David McKitterick (New York: Moretus Press, 1979), p. 112.

Notes to pages 28–40

I would like to thank the Harvard University Archives for permission to quote from materials in its collections.

1. *Secretary's Sixth Report Harvard College Class of 1893* (Cambridge: The Class, 1918), pp. 314–15.
2. For details of the Wideners' donations see William Bentinck-Smith, "The Passing of Gore and the Building of Widener: A Documentary Tale," in his *Building a Great Library: The Coolidge Years at Harvard* (Cambridge, Mass.: Harvard University Library, 1976), pp. 69–103.
3. On Livingston, see George Parker Winship, "Luther S. Livingston: A Biographical Sketch," *Papers of the Bibliographical Society of America* 8 (1914): 109–20, and the following bibliography of Livingston's separate publications, pp. 121–34. The biographical sketch and bibliography were also issued as a separate, reprinted from the Society's *Papers*, and the sketch alone in a limited edition of 200 copies printed by the Montague Press as *Luther S. Livingston, 1864–1914* (Cambridge, Mass., April 1915).
4. Harvard University Archives (call no. HUG 4879.8); hereafter HUA.
5. HUA (call no. HUG 4879.8).
6. HUA (call no. HUG 4879.6).
7. HUA (call no. HUG 4879.5).
8. HUA (call no. HUG 4879.8).
9. Archibald Cary Coolidge, *Report of . . . Director of the University Library Including the Fourteenth Report of William Coolidge Lane, Librar-*

ian, Reprinted, with Additions, from the Report of the President of Harvard University for 1910–11 (Cambridge, Mass., 1911), p. 17. The first year the course was offered, only four students enrolled: two seniors and two graduate students.

10. HUA (call no. HUG 4879.5).

11. Coolidge to Winship, 19 Feb. 1915, and Winship to Coolidge, 20 Feb. 1915; HUA (call no. HUG 4879.5).

12. *Division of Fine Arts 1915–16,* "Official Register of Harvard University," vol. XII, no. 1, pt. 17 (May 25, 1915), p. 17.

13. Lane to Winship, 27 Feb. 1915, HUA (call no. HUG 4879.5).

14. HUA (call no. HUG 4879.8). The course is also listed in the Radcliffe College catalogue from 1926 to 1933. From 1918 to 1930 and 1932 Winship also offered Fine Arts 20i, a graduate course with the same title in which many of his former FA 5e students enrolled. I am grateful to Jane Knowles, Mariana Oller, and Virginia L. Smyers for this information.

15. The list of students in Fine Arts 5e, based on "final returns" in HUA, was commenced by Virginia L. Smyers and completed by Mariana Oller. The course was not offered during the normal school year in 1918–19, probably due to disruption caused by the war, but an attendance slip (in the possession of the author) indicates that it was offered during the summer session in 1919 for five students: D.T. Eaton, Mrs. Mary E. Fisher, F. Hubbard, W.M.V. Hoffman, and F.G. White.

16. Douglas H. Gordon, "George Parker Winship," 9th George Parker Winship lecture, Houghton Library, 1978 (photocopy of typescript in possession of the author); Boies Penrose, "George Parker Winship" in *Grolier 75: A Biographical Retrospective* (New York: Grolier Club, 1959), pp. 185–87; Walter Muir Whitehill, "George Parker Winship, 1871–1952" in *Analecta Biographica: A Handful of New England Portraits* (Brattleboro: Stephen Greene Press, 1969), pp. 1–14; Arthur A. Houghton Jr., *Remembrances* (Queenstown, Md.: The Author, 1986), p. 134. For other accounts based on students' reminiscences see Roger E. Stoddard, "David P. Wheatland (1898–1993)," *Harvard Library Bulletin,* n.s. 4, no. 3 (Fall 1993): 5; David Farmer, *Stanley Marcus: A Life with Books* (Dallas: Still Point Press, 1993; rptd. Fort Worth: Texas Christian University Press, n.d. 1995), pp. 1–2, 4–5; Stoddard, *Teaching the History of Books at Harvard, 1910–1987/88* (Cambridge, Mass.: Harvard College Library, 1997), pp. 8–10

17. Penrose, "George Parker Winship," pp. 185–86.

18. Stoddard, "David P. Wheatland," p. 5.

19. Torrey to Winship, 26 May 1931, HUA (call no. HUG 4879.5).

20. Whitehill, "George Parker Winship," p. 10.

21. Winship, *Printing in the Fifteenth Century* (Philadelphia: University of Pennsylvania Press, 1940), p. [v].

22. Winship, *Fine Arts 5e Recommended Reading for 1931–1932* (Cambridge, 1932), p. [3]; 4-page leaflet in the possession of the au-

thor. In offering this list, Winship explains that this year "it was necessary to pass over nearly everything between the years of 1480 to 1730" (p. [2]).

23. Winship, *Fine Arts 5e Recommended Reading*, pp. [3–4].

24. Fine Arts 5e printed examination slips, originals in the possession of the author with the exception of that for 1925 (Harvard College Library, call no. B 5105.15.2).

25. Winship, *Dunster House: A College Book Shop* (Cambridge, Mass., 1919); 8-page leaflet in the possession of the author.

26. A Former Student [Gustave Pabst], *A Letter to the Students of The History of the Printed Book . . . Fine Arts 5e at Harvard College* (Cambridge, Mass.: Sign of the George, 1922), pp. [4–5]; 8-page leaflet in possession of the author is inscribed by Pabst, as author, to Winship. Pabst's letters (all presumably from 1922) concerning the prize are in HUA (call no. HUG 4879.5, folder of undated material). The prize book for 1922–23 was awarded to David P. Wheatland; see Stoddard, "David P. Wheatland," p. 5.

27. *Division of Fine Arts 1915–16*, "Official Register of Harvard University," vol. XII, no. 1, pt. 17 (May 25, 1915), p. 17.

28. These and other reports are in HUA (call nos. for those mentioned are HUC 8928.328.5.37, HUC 8929.328.5.8, HUC 8930.328.5.48, HUC 8931.3.328.5.7, HUC 8931.328.5.20, respectively).

29. HUA (call no. HUG 4879.5).

30. For details see correspondence in HUA (call no. HUG 4879.12). One colorful account of the cause of friction is in Gordon, "George Parker Winship," though interestingly Winship's teaching clearly also troubled Mrs. Rice. In an undated draft letter to Mrs. Rice (presumably written in Oct. 1925), Winship explains: "You have said recently that you do not carecabout [sic] my teaching. Neither do I, for it interferes with other things I would much rather do. But the only time I had a long talk with Harry Elkins Widener, he said that there ought to be a course such as I now give, at Harvard; that he wished ne [i.e. he] might have had such a course and spoke of the possibility of my giving it; and he spoke of ways in which he could help to make this a reality. In recollection of that talk, it seems to me that this teaching is the best thing I can do for his memory."

31. For a brief sketch of the Sign of the George and checklist of its imprints to 1929 see Will Ransom, *Private Presses and Their Books* (New York: Bowker, 1929), pp. 117–18, 289–90.

32. *John Barnard and His Associates* (Cambridge, Mass., 1927), p. [23].

33. A number of these are in the possession of the author. See also Penrose, "George Parker Winship," pp. 186–87, and Whitehill, "George Parker Winship," pp. 12–13.

34. William H. Bond, "The John Barnard Associates and the George Parker Winship Lectures," in A.N.L. Munby, *The Earl and the*

Thief, First George Parker Winship Lecture, 1 May 1968 (Cambridge, Mass.: Houghton Library, n.d. 1968), p. iv. Instrumental in establishing and raising funds for these lectures was Eric Hyde Lord Sexton, a student in Fine Arts 5e in 1928–29.

35. HUA (call no. HUG 4879.5).

36. Robert Pierpont Blake & Walter Benjamin Briggs, *Harvard University Library Annual Report for the Year 1936–37* (Cambridge, 1937), p. 1; Keyes DeWitt Metcalf, *Harvard University Library Annual Report for the Year 1937–38* (Cambridge, 1938), p. 337.

37. Letter in possession of the author.

38. Stoddard, *Teaching the History of Books*, p. 9.

39. George H. Sargent, "Making the New Book Collectors," *Publishers' Weekly*, 21 March 1925, p. 1112.

Harvard Students

in George Parker Winship's Fine Arts 5e.
Taken from Records in the Harvard University Archives.
By Mariana S. Oller, Curatorial Assistant, Rare Books Department,
Houghton Library.

1915–16
R. B. Brown
M. Martin
K. B. Murdock
R. C. Seamans
J. E. Towne
S. T. Williamson
N. B. Clark

1916–17
J. R. Busk
R. N. Cram
J. G. Heinz
R. C. Kelley
W. H. Meeker
W. W. Sanders
L. S. Schwartz
G. W. Tobin
E. A. Whitney
R. D. Williams

1917–18
W. S. Burrage
W. Burry
D. Davis
P. V. Donovan
L. F. Eames
W. F. Fogg
G. H. Pulsifer
Richard Roelofs
H. I. Wilkins
W. R. Swart

1919 Summer School
David T. Eaton
Ford Hibbard
W. M. Hoffman Jr.
Frederick Glover White

1919–20
H. E. Andrews
C. F. Batchelder
E. B. Brady
A. W. Closson
H. P. Edwards
P. C. Francis
G. Gade
L. Hunt
W. R. Morse
Stuart Osgood
H. B. Sluigerland
L. B. Van Ingren
N. H. White

1920 Summer School
P. A. Brickley
C. D. Case
R. Currier
E. B. Duncan
C. Hunneman Jr.
E. Lovering Jr.
L. Macfarland
R. Miller
W. V. Miller
G. C. Noyes

1920–21
J. Alger
C. H. Baldwin
J. C. Baldwin
H. G. Crosby
H. W. Hodgdon
S. Huckins
E. C. Lovett
H. S. Morgan
G. Pabst
F. T. Pfaelzer
C. A. Ross
D. Wright

1921–22
C. F. Allen
A. F. Anderson
H. K. Behn
G. W. Crist
G. P. Fogg
G. O. Forrest
A. B. Hamilton
A. T. Kent
M. E. Lord
G. A. Maddox
D. D. Miller
P. L. Romaine
P. L. Saltonstall
G. H. Shattuck
C. H. Smith
J. B. Stillwell
A. G. Tuckerman

1922–23
Sherlock Davis
D. Dunscombe
H. R. Hoyt
K. A. S. Safe
H. J. Schiesswohl
F. deN. Schroeder

W. E. Stearns
R. F. Thayer
J. K. Watson
D. P. Wheatland
C. B. Monro

1923–24
Grosvenor Bemis
J. S. Borg
H. L. Cole
A. B. Davis
W. B. Duncan
William Ehrlich
Adrien Gambet
G. T. Goodspeed
D. H. Gordon
L. F. Harris
M. A. Hay
B. Mck. Henry
J. S. Lincoln
Donald McVickar
Charles Marx
J. P. Monks
J. R. P. Nason
E. C. Parker
H. W. Reid
E. W. Stevens

1924–25
L. M. Beebe
D. B. Bianchi
J. P. Duncan
Darragh Louderback
H. E. Magill
H. S. Marcus
C. C. Mason
Arthur Menken
L. M. Millard
J. A. O'Connor
J. H. G. Pell

Boies Penrose
W. W. Scott
L. H. Sherrill
M. L. Stout
R. E. Sumner
A. M. White
W. M. Whitehill

1925–26
A. R. Allen
W. A. M. Burden
S. F. Collier
A. G. Cooke
F. M. Davies
B. N. Everett
Bradley Fisk
M. B. Glick
J. W. Lane
Kent Leavitt
H. H. MacCubbin
W. I. Nichols
R. T. Paine
F. W. Perkins
J. T. Pratt
C. A. Smart
John Trounstine
Paul Vanderbilt
D. B. Wilson

1927–28
Bailey Aldrich
M. L. Bell
D. W. Bethell
J. H. Browne
J. M. Curran
A. L. Devens
G. T. Francis
C. C. Gray
R. M. Hirsch
J. S. Jennison

G. L. Jones
L. E. Kirstein
T. D. Mumford
C. B. Otis
H. G. Payson
C. H. Pforzheimer
H. H. Proctor
J. I. Shaw
B. M. Starks
Whitney Stone
R. H. Weatherhead
E. A. Wieser
Craig Wylie

1928–29
Robeson Bailey
J. M. Barnes
J. M. Barnum
W. C. Bidlack
P. M. Brody
J. R. Carter
H. P. Chamberlin
B. S. Clark
J. DeNormandie
J. G. Douglas
E. W. Fordyce
R. R. Forrester
V. M. Fry
G. S. Greene
R. B. Harkness
P. S. Harris
Reed Harwood
Paul Henle
Mark Hopkins
A. A. Houghton
H. F. Hurlburt
W. E. Hutton
J. R. Murdoch
Beaumont Newhall
John Parkinson

D. C. Percival, Jr.
F. R. Rahr
R. P. Read
H. H. Richardson
A. P. Rogers
R. H. L. Sexton
F. L. Spalding
R. R. Stebbins
B. W. Stevens
R. A. Stewart
H. H. Sutherland
W. D. Taylor
G. O. B. Ulman
J. W. Valentine
P. P. Wadsworth
C. T. Wheeler
W. T. Wetmore
Eugene Williams
R. B. Williams
F. S. Wright
W. F. Wyeth

Graduates
W. K. Covell
A. D. Fuller
Philip Hofer
C. A. Rubel
Peter Wolfe

1929–30
C. F. Adams
W. N. Bates
Julius Birge
Kirk Bond
R. J. Bulkley
S. W. Burchard
J. M. Byrne
Henry Chalfant
O. S. Chute
G. F. Flavin

Ogden Goelet
J. L. Grandin
Theodore Hall
Amor Hollingsworth
J. D. Kidd
W. A. C. Miller
James Parker
N. E. Parkinson
G. J. Pick
Marshall Rawle
T. L. Robinson
T. N. Rogers
James Roosevelt
C. D. Stillman
W. D. Ticknor
H. D. Walker
E. M. M. Warburg
F. M. Weld
F. L. Winston

1930–31
S. L. Batchelder
Philip Boyer
L. C. Briggs
Paul Brooks
R. G. Coburn
Charles Devens
John Drum
Byron Elting
C. Flaccus
Robert Gilmor
R. M. Kellogg
R. D. Kernan
A. D. Langmuir
R. K. Leonard
W. F. Lutz
F. S. Nicholas
Geoffrey Parsons
L. F. Percival
H. T. Peters

B. E. Pollak
Beekman Pool
Donough Prince
Evan Randolph
St. John Smith
J. B. Stetson
S. W. Swaim
W. B. Trafford
H. T. Wagstaff
Eustis Walcott
M. D. Wheelock
Thomas Whiteside
E. M. Worthen
H. S. Young

1931–32
R. W. Baker
K. G. F. Balfour
R. H. Bates
Holland Bennett
J. K. Bottomley
A. L. Castle
Ephron Catlin
Walter Channing

Eugene DuBois
T. B. Eastland
J. C. Hagerty
Horace Hart
J. B. Hawes
P. W. Herrick
S. D. King
G. H. Kinnicutt
Caslon Lewis
R. B. Minturn
J. K. Mitchell
R. G. Mitchell
A. L. Nickerson
H. G. Nickerson
W. B. Pattee
H. W. Poett
C. P. Richardson
S. S. Sands
H. T. Swain
T. M. Torrey
R. T. Wharton
P. M. Whitman
H. W. Williams

Radcliffe Students

in George Parker Winship's Fine Arts 5e.
Taken from Records in the Radcliffe Archives.
By Mariana S. Oller, Curatorial Assistant, Rare Books Department,
Houghton Library.

1926–27
Mary E. Bowler AB28
Flora M. Burt AB29 (30 as of 29)
Eleanor C. Chilson AB27
Adelaide Hammond AB29 (Mrs. Edwin G. Johnson)
Lillian J. Horton AB29 (Mrs. Hubert T. Nelson)
Marion G. McQuesten AB28

1927–28
Jane E. Curtis N26-27 (Mrs. John A. Parker)
Margaret E. Gilman AM16
Marian Kelleran Harris AB21 (Mrs. Charles W. Phinney)
Harriet Nye AB30 (Mrs. Leo Gans)
Bernice Park AB29 (Mrs. Paul E. Jones)
Eleanor H. Pattee AB28 (Mrs. Harry E. Warren)
Agnes Shields AB28
Hetty L. Shuman

1928–29
Louise Bradley AB30
Ruth Dawson AB30
Helen Frances Devlin AB30
Doris B. Duley AB29 (Mrs. William Baumrucker)
Katherine Field Ehrgott AB28 (Mrs. James R. Caldwell)
Edith R. Elder AB29
Katharine P. Ernst AB30 (Mrs. Wallace H. Wulfeck)
Fay Goell AB29 (Mrs. Fay London)
Ruth A. Klivans AB30 (Mrs. Max Krauss)
Carol J. Koehler N27-30 (Mrs. Carl H. Pforzheimer Jr.)
Frances W. Luce AB30 (Mrs. John H. Clarke)
Phyllis E. McCausland AB29 (Mrs. Burke Rivers)
Virginia E. Morse AB29 (Mrs. Allen G. Shepherd Jr.)

Sylvia F. G. Mussells AB30 (Mrs. Eric M. Lindsay)
Mary E. Parke AB29
Eleanor Peterson AB30 (Mrs. Donald J. Finlayson)
Katherine I. Quine AB29 (Mrs. Oren A. Armstrong)
Sarah Roberts AB29
Jeanette E. Smith N27-30 (Mrs. Warham W. Janes)
Florence Wellington Swan AB99 G28-29
    (Mrs. Samuel S. Montague)
Celia Vandermark AB30 (Mrs. Mason Scudder)
Sara White AB29 (Mrs. Aaron G. Goldberg)
Marian H. Winter N27-29
Virginia Woodward AB29 (Mrs. John P. Dickson)

1929–30
Ruth-Marie Ballard AB29
Frances Anderson Boyd
Juliet MCC Browne AB30 (Mrs. Charles A. Boynton)
Ethel C. Dansie AB31 (Mrs. Theodore T. Ayers)
Dorothy Dean AB31 (Mrs. James S. Van Leuvan)
Frances Rowe Fleming AB30 (Mrs. Walter L. Chapin Jr.)
Florence M. Friedholm AB30
Eleanor Frothingham AB30 (Mrs. Austin Smith)
Madeleine Harding
Katharine Maynard
Louise Rosenfield AM33 (Mrs. Maurice H. Noun)
Dorothy B. Stanton AB30 (Mrs. Otto F. G. Schilling)
Esther S. Sweet
Mary Van Fleet AB30 (Mrs. Roger T. Waite)
Ruth Edith Volk AB30 (Mrs. Bernard S. Barenberg)
Corlis Keturah Wilber AB30 (Mrs. Richard G. Abell)

1930–31
Aurora Laurice Ball AB31 (Mrs. Willis N. Cousins)
Clara Butler AB31 (Mrs. Arnold A. Archibald)
Aileen B. Cohen AM31 (Mrs. Erich P. Frank)
Priscilla Ferguson G30-31
Amelia Worthington Fisk AB32 (Mrs. Brenton K. Fisk)
Gertrude E. Hatfield AB31 (Mrs. Graham T. Coulter)
Ruth L. Hay AB31
Jean Wesson Murray AB31

Florence M. Prussian N29-31 (Mrs. P. H. Bornstein)
Edith Thacher AB33 (Mrs. Clement Hurd)

1931–32

Phebe Anne Alden AB32 (Mrs. Everett A. Tisdale)
Barbara F. Brintnall AB32 (Mrs. Edward E. Simpson)
Margaret Alice Cole AB32 (Mrs. M. Cole Savage)
Diane Cummings AB32 (Mrs. Diane Beattie)
Ruth Carolyn Dromms AB32 (Mrs. Thomas D. Black)
Margaret Ford AB32 (Mrs. Edward L. Francis)
Marion B. Freeman AB32 (Mrs. Benjamin W. Porter)
Caroline Gleick AM32 (Mrs. Arthur H. Rosene)
Carolyn E. Jakeman AB32
Sarah L. Jenkins AB32 (Mrs. William H. Machale)
Ruth I. Kingsbury AB32 (Mrs. S Brainard McCarthy)
Ethel Inez Klein AB32 (Mrs. Frank Newton)
Gertrude Marion McGill AB32
Rosemary Rita McHugh AB33 (Mrs. George M. Nicholson)
Madge M. Matheny N30-31 (Mrs. Franklin E. Rice)
Carol Newcomb AB32 (Mrs. Charles B. Emde)
Margaret C. Osgood AB34
Laura M. L. Speyers
Harriet Eaton Weatherbee AB31 (Mrs. Leslie H. Thompson)
Ruth Baker Wellington AB33 (Mrs. Francis G. Shaw)
Isabelle Harriet Whittle G31-32 (Mrs. J. M. Cooper-Smith)
Nancy Tarlton Wright AB32 (Mrs. Andrew B. Small)

1932–33

Eleanor Clarke Balmer AM33 (Mrs. Victor Orsini)
Elvira Ogden AB33 (Mrs. Robert T. Young Jr.)
Nancy D. Patten AB32 (33 as of 32) (Mrs. Frank E. South)
Ann R. Smeltzer AB33

The following owners have allowed reproduction here: George Parker Winship Junior of his oil painting of the young Winship and his photograph of Winship in the Widener Room; Michael Winship of his Winship bookplate and photograph of Winship in the John Carter Brown Library; the John Carter Brown Library of its photograph of the oil portrait of Winship as a young man and its photograph of Winship in the Brown house library; and Martin Hutner of his imprints from the Sign of the George. The rest of the illustrations are taken from originals in the Harvard College Library.

DESIGN: Greer Allen

TYPESETTING: John J. Moran

TEXT PRINTING: The Stinehour Press

ILLUSTRATIONS: E. H. Roberts Company

BINDING: Mueller Trade Bindery